HOW TO BE A KNOW-IT-ALL ON ALMOST ANY SUBJECT YOU CAN THINK OF

by Hena Khan

SCHOLASTIC INC.

New York Toronto London Auckland Sydney

Mexico City New Delhi Hong Kong Buenos Aires

ISBN: 0-439-57907-4

Design: Julie Mullarkey Gnoy, Robert Rath
Illustrations: Kelly Kennedy

Copyright © 2004 by Scholastic Inc.

All rights reserved. Published by Scholastic Inc.

SCHOLASTIC, HOW TO SURVIVE ANYTHING, and associated logos
are trademarks and/or registered trademarks of Scholastic Inc.

12 11 10 9 8 7 6 5 4 3 2 1   4 5 6 7 8 9/0

Printed in the U.S.A.

First Scholastic printing, August 2004

CONTENTS

How to Survive This Book

Wait a minute. You might be thinking, "**Know-it-all**? Isn't that an insult?" Well, okay, you *might* have been called a know-it-all before by someone who thought you were being bossy: that is, you always seem to have an answer for everything. At the time, it probably didn't feel so great to be called one. That's because the odds are good that whoever said it didn't mean it in a congratulatory way, like, *"Wow! You're so amazing! You know it all!"* But, that's all about to change. **You're about to transform the term "know-it-all" into something to be proud of—and something everyone will want to be.** No kidding!

Think about it—isn't it a good thing to know a lot about a whole lot of stuff (even if not quite everything)? Of course it is! Because, just like another great know-it-all once said, **"Knowledge is power."** * And the more knowledge you have, the more powerful you are! Not in a more-powerful-than-a-locomotive kind of way, but in a dazzle-people-with-your-intellect kind of way, in a not-being-taken-advantage-of kind of way, in a being-a-person-who-feels-confident-and-smart kind of way—in short, in being a know-it-all in a *good* kind of way!

So, how is this big transformation going to happen? Well, starting off with this book, of course! **You won't end up knowing quite everything about everything, but you'll know a lot more than you do right now.** Stuff like, for instance, how your body works, where in the world you are, what the largest ocean is, the coldest place on Earth, and much more! Some of it might even be stuff that you've been taught before in school, but somehow managed to snooze through (because it wasn't *nearly* as exciting as it will be here!). Or stuff that you remembered just long enough for your next quiz. But you'll want to hold on to what you learn here, because it's useful, fun, and will make you the know-it-all you want to be!

* That know-it-all was **Sir Francis Bacon**, English philosopher and all-around smart guy, who said those famous words back in 1597!

Word Power!

This month you've got an exciting and challenging game called **Word Sense**™ that'll help you be the biggest know-it-all around!
With Word Sense, you'll become a speedy thinker and find new ways to come up with words you never even knew you knew!

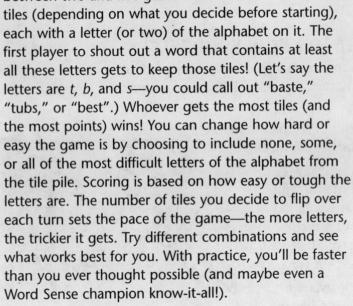

The game works like this: you and your opponent take turns flipping over anywhere between two and five game tiles (depending on what you decide before starting), each with a letter (or two) of the alphabet on it. The first player to shout out a word that contains at least all these letters gets to keep those tiles! (Let's say the letters are *t*, *b*, and *s*—you could call out "baste," "tubs," or "best".) Whoever gets the most tiles (and the most points) wins! You can change how hard or easy the game is by choosing to include none, some, or all of the most difficult letters of the alphabet from the tile pile. Scoring is based on how easy or tough the letters are. The number of tiles you decide to flip over each turn sets the pace of the game—the more letters, the trickier it gets. Try different combinations and see what works best for you. With practice, you'll be faster than you ever thought possible (and maybe even a Word Sense champion know-it-all!).

How Well Do You Know Yourself?

So you think you know yourself pretty well, huh? Oh *sure*, you know what size clothes you wear, and you can guess what time your stomach will start gurgling before lunch! You probably even remember the last time you were sick enough to skip school, and whether or not you're *really* allergic to brussel sprouts. But, **how many amazing and obscure facts about your body do *you* actually know?** Find out with this "Get to Know Yourself!" quiz.

Can you tell if the following statements are totally true or completely made up?

GET TO KNOW YOURSELF!

- A sneeze can rip out of your mouth at the super-speed of 100 miles per hour!

- There are more nerve cells in your brain than there are stars in our galaxy!

- Your body contains eight pints of blood, and is made up of 70 percent water.

- The average person has six pounds of skin.

- Your earwax is sticky enough to trap dust, and even *bugs*!
- The gurgling sound your stomach makes has a scientific name—*borborygmus*!
- You blink about 84,000,000 times a year.
- Your eyelashes last 150 days before falling out.

- Your face uses 14 muscles to smile and 43 to frown.
- By the time you're an adult, you'll have five million hairs all over your body—about the same amount as a gorilla!
- You produce about a quart of saliva every day—which adds up to 10,000 gallons in your lifetime!
- Your stomach creates a new layer of mucus every two weeks to prevent it from digesting itself.

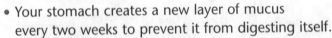

Find it hard to believe that you have the same amount of body hair as a giant monkey? Well, grab a banana, because that, along with every other statement in the quiz, is absolutely, one hundred percent true! By the way, in case you're wondering how it's possible that you're as hairy as Bubbles the Chimp, your hairs are so super-fine, they're more difficult to see than the ones on a chest-beating, flea-picking, tree-swinging gorilla! **Your body is truly the most complex, scientifically advanced, and sometimes bizarre machine known to humans.** Simply put, there's *nothing* else like it in the world.

WHAT'S IN YOUR HEAD?

Without your brain, you wouldn't be much of a know-it-all—in fact, you wouldn't know, feel, or think anything at all! **Your brain is what's in charge of everything you do, since it's what gives the rest of your body orders—from when to sneeze, sweat, and snooze, to how to stand on your head, solve a riddle, and run after the bus.** So, how well do you know your noodle? Take the Who's the Boss? quiz up next, and test your brain smarts!

ACTION!

DIRECTOR

POP QUIZ — WHO'S THE BOSS?

1. Your brain is:

   a. perfectly smooth and shaped like an onion

   b. bumpy, like the top of your tongue

   c. squishy, wrinkly, and wet

2. Your brain is about as firm as:

   a. a stick of butter

   b. a well-done steak

   c. a rock

3. By the time you grow up, your brain will be as big as:

   a. a walnut

   b. a lemon

   c. a grapefruit

4. Your brain goes to sleep when:

   a. you sleep

   b. you daydream

   c. never

5. Your brain tells the rest of your body what to do through:

a. e-mail

b. secret code

c. 10 billion nerve cells that send signals to the rest of your body

6. The *cerebrum*, the biggest part of your brain, has:

a. microchips

b. two sides

c. four sides

7. Your brain is made up mostly of:

a. protein

b. water

c. fat

8. Your brain is bigger than:

a. a gorilla's brain

b. any other mammal's brain on Earth

c. any other creature's brain on Earth

9. People with large heads have:

a. the largest brains

b. the smallest brains

c. big heads—and the same-sized brain as anyone else!

Check your answers on the next page, and give yourself **one point** for every one you get correct. How do you measure up?

6–9 points = The Main Brain!

3–5 points = You're Almost a Brainiac!

0–2 points = Brain Freeze!

Answers

1. **c.** Your brain isn't the most beautiful-looking thing, but it *is* powerful! The brain is soft and squishy, with lots of wrinkles and folds, and kind of resembles the inside of a walnut in shape.

2. **a.** Even though it's the most powerful thing in your body, your brain is as soft as butter!

3. **c.** The average brain weighs about three pounds and is the size of a grapefruit. That's only about two percent of the average person's body weight!

4. **c.** Your brain never rests! Even when your body is asleep, your brain is hard at work, telling your heart to keep beating, your lungs to breathe, and the rest of your body to keep busy digesting, growing—and everything else.

5. **c.** Your brain is like a gigantic mission control—it sends out thousands of signals to the rest of your body through nerve cells, which tell your body what to do!

6. **b.** The cerebrum, which makes up 85 percent of the brain, is divided into two sides, left and right. Scientists believe that the right side of the brain helps you think creatively, and enjoy things like music and colors. The left side of the brain is believed to help you think analytically, and do things like math and logic.

7. **b.** Like the rest of your body, your brain is made up mostly of water—more than 70 percent, in fact! The rest is made of protein and fat.

THIS IS A WHALE OF A GOOD TIME!

8. **a.** Although the human brain isn't the largest one on Earth, it's the most powerful. A sperm whale's brain is a bit larger than a human's—but think about how much bigger a whale is than you! A human brain makes up a bigger *percentage* of the body than any other animal. A gorilla, which is the animal most like a human, has a brain only about a *third* of the size of a human brain.

9. **c.** A bigger head doesn't mean a bigger brain!

THAT MAKES SENSES!

Sure, you can brag about your awesome brain to the rest of the animal kingdom, but what some other critters lack in brainpower, they make up with incredible super-senses. Imagine having these extraordinary abilities to **see**, **hear**, **taste**, **smell**, and **feel**!

- Each eye of a **chameleon** can move in a different direction—that means it can see in opposite directions at the same time!

- An **eagle** can see three times better than a human—its eyeballs are about a third bigger than yours!

- A **pig**, even though it eats just about *anything*, has 15,000 taste buds on its tongue, compared to the 9,000 you have.

HELLO? HELLO?

- A **cricket** can hear with its *legs*, since sound waves vibrate a special membrane on them!

- **Mice** can hear frequencies between 1,000 and 100,000 hertz, while humans can only hear the ones between 20 and 20,000 hertz (a *hertz* is a unit that measures frequencies of sound).

- A **snake's** tongue doesn't have any taste buds at all! Instead, it collects specks in the air, water, or ground to bring taste and smell into its mouth.

- Some **spiders** have as many as eight eyes (which makes it pretty amazing that you can ever squash one!).

- A **falcon** can see its prey clearly from far away—even when diving to grab it at 100 miles per hour!

I'M OUTTA HERE!

- The **star-nosed mole** has six times more touch receptors in its fleshy nose (which it uses to dig for food) than the human hand!

How Does Your Brain Measure Up?

ANIMAL	SIZE OF BRAIN (IN GRAMS)
Sperm whale	7,800
Elephant	6,000
Adult human	**1,300–1,400**
Newborn baby (human)	350–400
Orangutan	370
Lion	240
Dog	72
Cat	30
Squirrel	7.6
Guinea pig	4

ARE YOU A HAIR-BRAIN?

Okay, so now you know all about the goings-on inside your head. But what about the stuff on *top* of it—your hair! For some unknown reason, when it comes to their beloved locks, a lot of people think they know it all. The truth is there are a lot of weird theories about how hair grows and falls out. Can you tell the difference between what's a hairy truth and what's a hairy myth?

1. It's perfectly normal to lose between 80 and 100 hairs a day, every day.

2. Brushing your hair a hundred times before bed every night will make it healthier.

I DON'T KNOW WHY MY MOM SAYS I NEED A HAIRCUT!

3. Your hair grows at a rate of about an inch every two months.

4. If you pull a gray hair out of your head, two will grow back in its place.

5. People inherit baldness from their mother's side of the family—which means that if your mom's dad is bald, and you're a boy, you will be bald too, when you grow up!

6. You can wake up with gray hair one morning.

7. Hair grows faster in the summer than in the winter.

8. The more often you cut your hair, the faster it will grow.

9. Wearing a hat all the time will make you go bald faster.

10. Eating poorly can cause your hair to fall out more than usual.

Answers

1. **True.** But don't worry—you have over 100,000 hair follicles on your head to make up for the lost hair.

2. **Myth.** Too much brushing can actually make your hair break! Don't toss the brush altogether—just stop when you're tidy (and why would you brush your hair before sleeping, anyway?).

3. **True.** That's about six inches a year!

4. **Myth.** Pulling any color hair out of your head means having one less hair on your head, until another one grows in. Think about it: if this were true, wouldn't almost-bald people just keep pulling out the hairs they had left to make more?

5. **Myth.** Baldness can be inherited from either parent, or just about any relative you have.

6. **Myth.** Getting gray hair is a long process, not something that happens overnight.

7. **True.** It's true, although no one is exactly sure why.

8. **Myth.** Cutting your hair only makes it shorter, and doesn't speed up the rate it grows back.

9. **Myth.** Nope! You may notice more bald people wearing hats, but they were probably bald first!

10. **True.** Poor nutrition affects many things about your body, including your hair.

How Well Do You Know the World?

Being a good know-it-all means knowing everything about the world you live in. Fine, maybe not *everything*—but probably a whole lot more than you know right now! That means getting to know the ins and outs, the ups and downs—and everything in between—about the planet we call home sweet home!

HAVE NO FEAR, IT'S A HEMISPHERE!

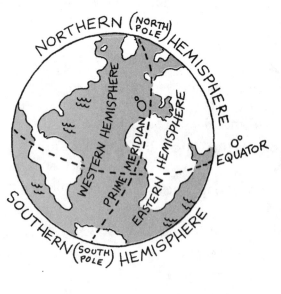

The most basic way people have decided to keep track of the world is to divide it up into four sections, known as the **hemispheres**. The hemispheres are formed by two imaginary lines drawn across the Earth—the **equator**, which runs from side to side around the Earth's belly like a belt, and the **Prime Meridian**, which goes from top to bottom. Everything above the equator is in the **Northern Hemisphere**, and everything below it is in the **Southern Hemisphere**. Everything to the east of the Prime Meridian is in the **Eastern Hemisphere** and—you guessed it, everything to the west is in the **Western Hemisphere**. Sounds simple enough? It is! But...

DID YOU KNOW THAT:

- People living in the Southern Hemisphere (like Australia) celebrate Christmas during the summertime?

- If you live in the Northern Hemisphere, you can see the North Star, but not if you live in the Southern Hemisphere? (The "North Star" of the Southern Hemisphere is the Southern Cross.)

- Even though the United States and Europe are often called the "West," Europe is actually in the Eastern Hemisphere?

- Whether you live in the Northern or Southern Hemisphere doesn't affect which direction the water in your toilet flushes?

- Most of the people of the world live in the Northern Hemisphere?

- The Winter Olympics have *always* been held in the Northern Hemisphere?

- All penguins live in the Southern Hemisphere (and there are none on the North Pole!)?

- The largest iceberg is found in the Southern Hemisphere and is roughly the size of the state of *Rhode Island?*

THE BIG SEVEN

In addition to whatever hemisphere you're standing on, you also live on a **continent**. You're probably thinking, *"Yeah, yeah, yeah, continents, shmontinents, I've heard it all before!"* Okay, smarty pants, how fast can you name them?

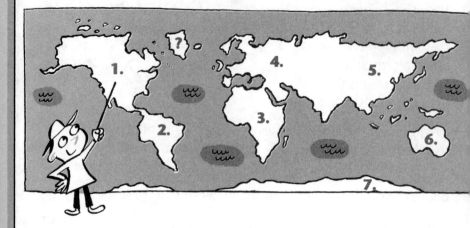

We're still *waiting*...all right,

THE SEVEN CONTINENTS ARE:

1. North America

2. South America

3. Africa

4. Europe

5. Asia

6. Australia

7. Antarctica

? As a true know-it-all, you would know that this island (which is not a continent) is Greenland.

Beyond their names, what else do you know about these land giants? Check out the upcoming quiz and see!

1. A "continental" breakfast consists of:

   a. bacon, eggs, toast, jam, and juice

   b. a flaky croissant and coffee

   c. dry cereal and milk

Just kidding! Although, in case you're wondering, a continental breakfast is a light breakfast of a pastry and coffee. It was named that by bigger-breakfast-eating British people who turned their noses up at the lighter fare preferred by folk on the rest of the European continent. With that little bit of trivia covered, here's the *real* quiz:

1. The only continent that has *3 billion* people living on it is:

   a. Africa

   b. Antarctica

   c. Asia

2. The only continent that's made up of a single country is:

   a. Africa

   b. Australia

   c. Antarctica

3. The continent that's divided up into the most countries is:

   a. Europe

   b. Africa

   c. South America

4. The only continent without *any* reptiles living on it is:

   a. North America

   b. Africa

   c. Antarctica

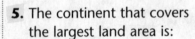

5. The continent that covers the largest land area is:

   a. Europe

   b. Asia

   c. North America

1. **c.** Asia wins hands down! There are over three times as many people living in Asia (most of them in China) than in the next most populated continent, Africa. And while often several thousand people live and work at scientific research stations in Antarctica—no one lives there permanently!

2. **b.** Only Australia is both a continent and a country. Antarctica isn't actually a country—it's a territory that isn't owned by anyone. Instead, a group of 40 countries share the territory for environmental research under what's known as the Antarctic Treaty System.

3. **b.** Africa has 53 countries in it, Europe has 43, and South America has 12.

4. **c.** That would be Antarctica! North America and Africa are both chock full of reptiles.

5. **b.** Asia is the largest continent on Earth.

Know-It-All Fact!

The existence of Antarctica wasn't confirmed until the 1800s! But, ancient Greek geographers were convinced that there was a large chunk of land around the South Pole to balance out the land they knew existed in the north (the Arctic, which you might know better as the North Pole). The Greeks even named the hypothetical land the opposite of the Arctic: the Anti-Arkitkos or Antarctica. And when it was finally discovered, the name stuck!

AROUND THE WORLD IN 80 DAYS

Your extremely lucky friend is on a world tour this summer, while you're stuck at regular old sleepaway camp, working your way through your second bottle of bug spray. **At least your friend has promised to send you a postcard from each country he visits.** And to add a little excitement, he's decided to leave out where he's writing from each time! Can you figure out where he is based on his clues?

A.

Hey there! I'm in a European country that's known for being shaped like an old boot. It's also famous for super-expensive cars like Ferrari and Lamborghini, and for little boats called gondolas. I've seen some really neat artwork

by Michelangelo and Leonardo Da Vinci, and I've eaten all kinds of pasta—but their pizza is still my favorite!
Where am I?

B.

It's me again! Now I'm in the country that Christopher Columbus thought he was headed to when he discovered the New World (talk about a mix-up!). Today, it's got the second largest number of people living in it in the world—and they speak over a hundred different languages! Women wear giant pieces of colorful cloth called "saris" that they wrap around their bodies like a dress. People here love to sing and dance and, believe it or not, almost all the movies made here are musicals. In fact, every year, almost twice the number of movies that are made in Hollywood are produced in this country's "Bollywood." I'm going to head to the movie theatre, and then have some lentils, spicy chicken curry, and rice for dinner. Maybe I'll follow it up with a walk along the Ganges River. **Where am I?**

C.

Wish you were here! I'm in the largest country in South America, and the only one where Portuguese is spoken. I'll have a chance to explore the largest rainforest in the world, and see monkeys, parrots, and all sorts of reptiles. I hope I don't run into any snakes! People here love to play soccer and this is the only country to have been in all of the soccer world cups (which is like the Super Bowl for soccer, worldwide). Where am I?

VENEZUELA
GUYANA
COLOMBIA
SURINAME
FRENCH GUIANA
ECUADOR
PERU
?
BOLIVIA
PARAGUAY
CHILE
ARGENTINA
URUGUAY

D.

Hey, what's up? This time I'm on an island country that's known as "the Land of the Rising Sun." I'm in the capital city, where I just got off one of the most crowded subway rides of my life! I had a tasty bowl of noodles at this neat restaurant where you take off your shoes, sit on the floor, and eat on a really low table. A little later, I'm going to meet my new friends for some karaoke. It was invented here, and people get really into it! They also really like video games, and some of the best ones are made here. I just hope I don't get lost again though, because I can't read any of the signs. I saw one today that looked like this: 成田空港 Where am I?

RUSSIA
MONGOLIA
CHINA
SOUTH KOREA
?
LAOS
VIETNAM
PHILIPPINES
CAMBODIA

E.

Hey again! I'm in the largest capital city in the world, which is sinking almost 10 inches a year! It's true—the city was built on a lake and has water pumped out of it for the millions of people living in it, which makes it sink. This is the country that introduced chocolate to the world, as well as some of my favorite food, like enchiladas and quesadillas. People speak Spanish and some wear big hats known as sombreros. The only bummer is the siesta—an afternoon naptime when everything closes for a few hours. I thought napping was for babies! But otherwise, I love it here. Where am I?

F.

Greetings! I'm in a country that has gone from being the home of mighty kings known as tsars, to a group of countries called the Soviet Union, to finally just one country about ten years ago. Today I saw St. Basil's Cathedral, which has nine domes in all! People here love to eat potatoes and bread. My favorite is blinies, thin pancakes filled with fish and other stuff. I've been staying away from the borscht (soup made from beets, bleh!). All the kids are really friendly here and say "Zdravstvuite" (which means "hello!"). I used my rubles to buy my sister some wooden Matrioshka dolls (which fit inside each other and go from biggest to really tiny). Where am I?

G.

What's shaking? I'm in a country that is both in Africa and Asia and was home to one of the oldest civilizations in history. Most of the country is desert and very HOT, which is why I'm staying in Cairo, a really crowded city along the Nile River. I've already gone to the bazaar (the marketplace) where everyone is selling anything you can imagine, and people argue over prices. I think I got a good deal on the stuffed camel toy I bought. When you press a button, it starts to sing—in Arabic! Tomorrow I'm going to see one of the most famous sites of the country, including the tombs of the ancient Pharaohs (where there used to be mummies inside—cool!). Where am I?

H.

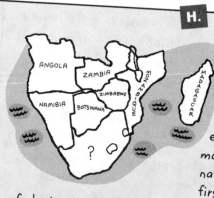

This is my last stop! I'm at the southern tip of a really neat continent, in the Southern Hemisphere!

It's a country that has a little of everything—white beaches, big modern cities, and best of all, national animal parks! I went on my first safari and took a lot of pictures of elephants, giraffes, zebras, and gazelles. I'm really enjoying the food here—everything from a hamburger to—amazingly—crocodile steaks and fried caterpillars!

Where am I?

Answers

A. Italy **B.** India

C. Brazil **D.** Japan

E. Mexico **F.** Russia

G. Egypt **H.** South Africa

22

WE ARE THE WORLD

What's the most important thing in the world? Why, *you*, of course (well you, and all the *other* people living on the planet!). How much do you know about the people you share the planet with?

1. How many people live on Earth with you?

   a. About 20 million

   b. Almost 2 billion

   c. More than 6 billion

2. What city has the most people living in it in the world (almost *12 million* people!)?

   a. Mumbai, India

   b. Hong Kong, China

   c. New York City, USA

3. How many languages do people speak in the world?

   a. More than 500

   b. More than 1,000

   c. More than 2,700

4. Which language is spoken the most in the world?

   a. Mandarin Chinese

   b. Spanish

   c. English

5. The world is divided up into how many different countries?

   a. Less than 100

   b. Between 100 and 150

   c. Over 150

1. **c.** The population of the world in 2004 is almost six and a half billion people, which is more than 20 times the number of folks living in the United States! There was an increase of almost a billion people living on our planet over the last ten years.

2. **a.** Although China is the country with the largest population (1.3 billion people!), India boasts the largest populated city in the world, Mumbai (formerly called Bombay).

3. **c.** Believe it or not, there are over 2,700 languages spoken in the world, and many more dialects (which are local variations of languages). Ever hear of Mponwe, Jita, or Wolof?

4. **a.** Mandarin Chinese! Over a billion people speak this language worldwide (mostly in China, though). English is the second most spoken language in the world, and is considered the international language, which is why so many people around the world try to learn it.

5. **c.** Although the number changes from time to time, there are currently 191 countries in the world.

How Low Can You Go?

Check out the highs and lows of your favorite planet—Earth!

- The **Himalayas**, in Nepal, are the world's **tallest mountains**.

- **Mauna Loa**, in Hawaii, is the Earth's **largest volcano** (don't worry, it's dormant, which means it won't be erupting any time soon!).

Welcome to the HIMALAYAS

- The **Dead Sea** (between Israel and Jordan) is the **lowest point** on Earth and is 1,350 feet below sea level.

- The **Nile** (in Egypt) is the **longest river** in the world—a whopping 4,000 miles long!

- **Mount Everest** is the **highest point** on land in the world at 29,035 feet.

- The **deepest point** that anyone has dug into the Earth is the **Western Deep mine** in South Africa—it goes 2.6 miles down into the ground!

- The **Pacific Ocean** is the **largest ocean** in the world, and more than twice as big as the next largest, the Atlantic.

- The **hottest place** on Earth is **Dallol, Ethiopia**, where the average temperature year round is 93.2 °F (34 °C).

- The **coldest place** on Earth is **Plateau Station, Antarctica**, where the average temperature is -70 °F (-56.7 °C).

- The **wettest place** on Earth is **Mawsynram, India**, where there is 467.4 inches of rainfall each year.

- The **driest place** is the **Atacama Desert, Chile**, where almost no measurable rain falls on a yearly basis.

- The **smallest island country** in the world is **Nauru**, located in the South Pacific. It's only about eight square miles!

Is the Dead Sea Really Dead?

Well, *you* decide! Unlike other bodies of water, filled with underwater creatures and plants, nothing lives in the Dead Sea (located between Israel and Jordan in the Middle East). Sound creepy? Well, it gets creepier: along the shores of the Dead Sea are white crystals of mineral salt that cover everything. And if fish accidentally swim into the sea from freshwater streams that feed into it, they die right away, and are washed ashore.

Luckily, the Dead Sea isn't so deadly for humans. The sea has been famous since ancient times because of its salty water and all the minerals in it, which people believe can actually keep them young and healthy. A number of spas and resorts exist along its shores, and Dead Sea products are sold all over the world. If you're ever in the area, why not go for a swim? It's easy, even if all you know is the "dead man's float," because *everything* floats in the Dead Sea (since the salty water is super-thick)!

It's a Small World After All

Even though the world has almost two hundred countries and six billion people living in it, there are a few super-famous structures that people anywhere in the world recognize. But here it's going to be a little trickier for you. You have to *guess* what these world-famous landmarks are, based on the clues!

1. I am an observation tower that was built in Europe in 1889. At that time, I was the tallest structure in the world at 986 feet high. I was made out of iron grids and was at first criticized by some people in my city for being ugly. But over time, I've become the most famous and loved symbol of Paris. **What am I?**

2. I am considered one of the most beautiful buildings in the world, made almost entirely of marble. My beauty is reflected by a gigantic pool that shows off my domes and pillars. I was built between 1631 and 1653, by an Indian ruler named Shah Jahan, to honor his wife, Mumtaz Mahal. It took almost 20,000 workers to build me. **What am I?**

3. I am 4,500 years old and the only one of the Seven Ancient Wonders of the World still standing. I am pointy, and made of more than two million blocks of stone that weigh 2.5 tons each! I was built entirely by hand, without any machines. I cover 13 acres of desert land and am 450 feet tall. I was built to be a tomb, but now I am a popular tourist site. **What am I?**

4. Soon after they began building me in Italy in 1173, my foundation started settling and I began to tilt. I was finally finished over 100 years later. Since 1912, I have continued to move 1.2 millimeters a year—but I haven't fallen over yet! My name gives a clue to what's been happening to me. **What am I?**

5. I was built over 2,000 years ago by Emperor Qin Shi Huangdi to keep out unwanted invaders. I stretch out over 4,500 miles (the distance between Miami and the North Pole!) and am between 15 and 30 feet high. Over three million people built me, over hundreds of years. I'm so big that I can be seen from space. **What am I?**

6. Over 45,000 bloodthirsty spectators used to gather inside my walls to watch gladiator games, in which people battled each other, or animals. You might have even seen something like me on the set of the movie *Gladiator*, with Russell Crowe. I have been the inspiration for modern stadiums around the world, even though I was built in Rome over 2,000 years ago. **What am I?**

7. I am the largest work of art on Earth, carved into a mountain. I was built by 400 workers to celebrate 150 years of American history starting in 1927. It took 14 years and $1 million to complete me. I have four famous faces that are each 60 feet high and look down on people from 500 feet above ground. **What am I?**

8. I was a gift from France to the United States back in 1884 to celebrate 100 years of independence from Britain. I stand tall at 305 feet, and greet people coming to New York City from all over the world. My arm is 30 feet long and holds a torch, and my official name is "Liberty Enlightening the World." **What am I?**

Answers

1. The Eiffel Tower, Paris, France
2. The Taj Mahal, Agra, India
3. The Great Pyramid of Giza, Egypt
4. The Leaning Tower of Pisa, Italy
5. The Great Wall of China, China
6. The Colosseum, Rome, Italy
7. Mount Rushmore, South Dakota, USA
8. The Statue of Liberty, New York, USA

WHAT'S YOUR STATE OF MIND?

Ready for a game? How about the game of *Jeopardy*? Grab an opponent and test your knowledge of the U.S. states (or play alone). Pick a category and a point level (the questions get harder as the points go higher). In each box, read the *answer* that's provided, and then give the right *question* that goes with it (like, "what is Oklahoma?"). Your turn continues as long as you get answers right. Keep track of the number of points you earn, and see who wins. Remember, you have to give your answers in the form of a question to get points. And here's a tip: each state only appears *once* in the game.

Point Level	Famous Monuments and Landmarks	Postal Codes	Famous People	State Nicknames	Other Random Stuff
100 points	The St. Louis arch is found here.	WV	Presidents George and George W. Bush are from this state, whose slogan is "Don't Mess with…". (name of the state)	The Sunshine State	This state is home of the famous car race, the Indianapolis 500.
200 points	The Liberty Bell is found here.	UT	Actor Arnold Schwarzenegger became governor of this state in 2004.	The Aloha State	This northeastern state is famous for making the most maple syrup in the country.
300 points	The Lincoln Memorial is found here.	AK	Hillary Clinton, the former First Lady, was elected Senator of this state.	The Peach State	This is the smallest state in the union.
400 points	The Sears Tower, the tallest building in the country, is in this state.	MN	Presidents George Washington, James Monroe, and Thomas Jefferson were all born here!	The Grand Canyon State	This state was purchased from Russia for $7 million in 1867.
500 points	The Wright Brothers Memorial honors the first people to ever fly an airplane here.	NE	Elvis Presley built his famous estate, known as Graceland, in this state.	The Mount Rushmore State	In this midwestern state, whose state capital shares its name, it's illegal to sleep on a refrigerator outdoors!

Answers

Point Level	Famous Monuments and Landmarks	Postal Codes	Famous People	State Nicknames	Other Random Stuff
100 points	What is Missouri?	What is West Virginia?	What is Texas?	What is Florida?	What is Indiana?
200 points	What is Pennsylvania? *(Philadelphia)*	What is Utah?	What is California?	What is Hawaii?	What is Vermont?
300 points	What is Washington, DC? (Okay, this one's not officially a state—but it's always listed with them!)	What is Arkansas?	What is New York?	What is Georgia?	What is Rhode Island?
400 points	What is Illinois? *(Chicago)*	What is Minnesota?	What is Virginia?	What is Arizona?	What is Alaska?
500 points	What is North Carolina? *(Kitty Hawk)*	What is Nebraska?	What is Tennessee?	What is South Dakota?	What is Oklahoma?

Keep the game going! Add the postal codes MD, VA, or NM, for example. Or try some more famous landmarks, like Yosemite National Park, and the Alamo. Do a little research and come up with your very own topics *and* answers!

Answers

MD: Maryland, VA: Virginia, NM: New Mexico, Yosemite National Park: California, Alamo: Texas

Here are two more mini-quizzes for you to stretch your brain and expand your *state* of mind!

A. The United States is divided up into four regions: the Northeast, the Midwest, the South, and the West. Can you point them out on this map?

B. What do you think are the largest cities (based on population) in the U.S.? Put them in the right order!

Chicago, Illinois

Los Angeles, California

Houston, Texas

New York, New York

Philadelphia, Pennsylvania

How Well Do You Know Your Way Around?

Now that you know a bit more about the way the world is set up, do you know where you really are? *Duh*, you know where you are right now, of course. But what if someone dropped you somewhere else on the planet. Could you find your way home? Think so? Well, here's the catch: you can't ask someone for directions, you can't look on the Internet—in fact, all you have is a (**gasp!**) map! *How well do you know your way around a map?* Well, soon enough, you'll know as much as the best of them!

For starters, every good map has a directional tool called a **compass rose** on it. That's the thing that looks like this.

The letters stand for **North**, **South**, **East**, and **West**. The idea is to point the map in the direction of north, and then follow it, right? But how do you know which way *is* north? *Aha!* That's where it gets tricky.

YOU CAN FIND NORTH BY:

- taking a blind guess and hoping you're right
- using a compass
- using your super know-it-all skills!

Blind guess? Um, no, that's not a smart idea! Using a compass? Sure, if you have one handy, it won't steer you wrong. A compass is basically a magnetized steel needle that spins around inside a case. It works because of the natural magnetic force of the Earth, which points the needle towards the North Pole. All you have to do is hold it flat on your hand, and turn your body until the needle lines up with the "N" and—*ta da*—you're facing north!

But, if you left home *without* your handy dandy compass, you can also rely on your new super know-it-all skills to figure out which way is north. Just read on!

BE A SUPERSTAR

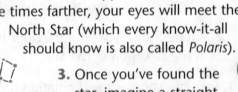

1. Look up into the sky and try to find a group of stars (or *constellation*) known as the Big Dipper. The stars are clustered in the shape of a big soup ladle, with three stars making the "handle," and four stars forming the "dipper."

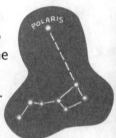

2. If you imagine that a line connecting the two stars at the front of the "dipper" extends out to a point five times farther, your eyes will meet the North Star (which every know-it-all should know is also called *Polaris*).

NORTH O
STAR

NORTH

3. Once you've found the star, imagine a straight line drawn from it to the Earth. That's north!

Know-It-All Fact!

Polaris is known as the North Star because it's almost directly above the North Pole at any time of the year. Contrary to what many people may think, it's *not* a very bright star, or the brightest star in the sky. That's why it helps to use the Big Dipper to find it.

Remember that stuff you learned about hemispheres? Well, if you're in the Southern Hemisphere, you can't ever see the North Star. So what's a poor lost know-it-all to do? Use the Southern Cross! It's made up of four stars that make a small cross in the southern sky. Imagine a line connecting the two stars that are farthest apart from each other in the Southern Cross. Then extend that line so that it's five times longer. From that imaginary point where that line ends, draw another line straight down to Earth. You've just found the direction south!

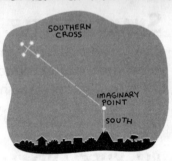

33

WATCH OUT!

Finding north with the stars doesn't always work. What if it's not nighttime? Then you can use your **watch**. You read that right—your watch! An *analog* watch (that means a watch with a face, not a digital one) can substitute as an emergency compass during the day. Here's how to make it work for you:

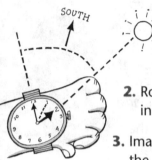

1. While standing outside, hold your watch face up (it can be strapped to your wrist, or you can hold it in the palm of your hand).

2. Rotate the watch until the hour hand points in the direction of the Sun.

3. Imagine another hand pointing halfway between the hour hand facing the Sun and the number 12 (like if the hour hand is on the 2, the imaginary hand would be halfway between 2 and 12, at 1).

4. The imaginary hand is pointing in the direction of south! If you turn to face south, the east is to your left, the west is to your right, and north is behind you. (If you're in the Southern Hemisphere, your imaginary hand will be pointing north!)

5. Now that you know which way is which, you can either head in the right direction, or if you have a map, point it the right way and follow it to get where you need to go!

SHAKE, RATTLE, AND ROLL!

How well do you know the stuff that rocks the planet? No, not music that you can get down and boogie to! We're talking about the serious movers and shakers here—tornadoes, earthquakes, tsunamis, and other stuff you *don't* want coming near you, no matter where you are!

I'LL HUFF, AND I'LL PUFF, AND I'LL BLOW YOUR HOUSE DOWN!

The big bad wolf? No, a **hurricane**! A hurricane is a tropical storm that is named when its winds scream along at 74 miles per hour, or faster. Hurricane winds can reach up to 190 mph, which is when they can destroy everything in their paths! What's the difference between a hurricane, **cyclone**, and a **typhoon**? Nothing! They're all different names for the same storms in different parts of the world.

Hurricanes don't get names like Carol, Gloria, or Bob just to be cute! Weather officials name hurricanes to keep track of them, especially since there can often be more than one brewing at a time. Hurricanes that cause the most destruction have their names retired (which means they can't be used again for the next ten years!).

LET'S DO THE TWIST!

When it's twister time, take cover! That's because "twister" is another word for **tornado**, a violently spinning cloud of winds that can speed along land at anywhere from 20 to 120 miles per hour! Unlike hurricanes, which hit coastal areas worst, tornadoes can strike anywhere at any time— although they're most common during the spring and early summer. Only about one percent of tornadoes are the deadliest kind—the ones that can pick up houses and drop them somewhere else (like in the land of Oz!). Although tornadoes are pretty uncommon everywhere else in the world, in the United States there are about 800 to 1,000 or more twisters a year. Tornadoes have been spotted in every state, during every month in the year. The highest concentration of tornadoes is in Oklahoma, Texas, and in Florida, while the lowest number are in Vermont, Alaska, and Rhode Island (where they rarely occur).

A REAL SHOCKER!

You know that during **thunderstorms**, it's good to stay away from open spaces and trees, which are most likely to be hit by lightning, and to keep indoors. Despite what you may have heard, the electric charge that rips through the sky *can* strike the same place twice (or even more) during a single storm!

At this very moment, there are about 1,800 thunderstorms taking place all over the world, and about 100 bolts of lightning strike the Earth each second! An average lightning flash could light a 100-watt light bulb for over three months (that's why you don't want to be anywhere near it!).

SHAKE IT UP!

Earthquakes are sudden vibrations that make the ground shake, and they're caused by the movement of the Earth's *crust* (the outer layer of the planet). As the crust bends and breaks, seismic waves are created, and they travel outward, making the ground shake. A *fault* is an area in the Earth's crust that moves and shifts, and it's a hot spot for earthquake activity. When two pieces of the crust collide into each other, or slide in opposite directions, an earthquake takes place.

There is a 100 percent chance of an earthquake taking place somewhere in the world today! It could be major, or even too small for anyone to feel, but since several *million* earthquakes take place each year, *thousands* take place each day. The biggest earthquakes don't always cause the most damage—it all depends on where they hit and how many people are around when they do.

HOT STUFF!

A **volcano** is an opening in the Earth's crust that pours out hot lava, broken rocks, ashes, dust, and gases from below the surface of the planet. Volcanoes can either be active (erupting now), dormant (not erupting right now, but capable of erupting later), or extinct (won't erupt again).

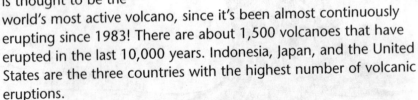

Kilauea, found in Hawaii, is thought to be the world's most active volcano, since it's been almost continuously erupting since 1983! There are about 1,500 volcanoes that have erupted in the last 10,000 years. Indonesia, Japan, and the United States are the three countries with the highest number of volcanic eruptions.

The word "volcano" comes from the ancient Roman god of fire, Vulcan. The most famous volcanic eruption of all time took place in Italy in A.D. 79. Mount Vesuvius buried the entire town of Pompeii and Herculaneum under 20 feet of ash and lava, killing an estimated 20,000 people, and preserving them. The ancient cities were uncovered in 1748, and excavation work still continues to this day.

WAVE RUNNER!

You don't want to surf on a **tsunami** (pronounced *sue-nah-me*)! These seismic sea waves are caused by underground earthquakes or volcanic activity, and they can travel in the open sea at speeds up to 450 miles per hour. When they near the coast, the waves can grow to be as high as 100 feet and smash into the shore, where they cause a lot of damage and destruction.

Tsunamis, named by the Japanese, are often incorrectly called tidal waves (but not by you, know-it-all!). Hawaii, Alaska, and Japan are at high risk for tsunamis. Two Tsunami Warning Centers exist in Honolulu, Hawaii, and Palmer, Alaska, that track changes on the Earth that could bring on a tsunami. They also issue warnings whenever possible. But warnings don't always work—in 2002, a tsunami hit in Indonesia, causing millions of dollars in damage and killing 1,000 people.

ARE YOU FOR REAL?

You've heard of some of the world's most famous myths, mysteries, and monsters. Some turned out to be fakes, but others are as real as you are! Here you'll find out which are which!

THESE ARE NOT REAL (EVEN THOUGH YOU MIGHT HAVE THOUGHT THEY WERE)!

Creature	Where You'll Find It	The Story
Leprechaun	Ireland	A leprechaun is a tiny fairy that looks like an old man. If you catch him, he'll lead you to a pot of gold. The trick is you have to keep looking at him. If he can get you to glance away, he'll vanish—and there goes your money!
Loch Ness Monster (Nessie)	Scotland	Since 1933, countless folk have claimed to have spotted, photographed, and videotaped a monster living in a lake known as Loch Ness, in North Central Scotland. They describe the monster as an enormous 30-foot-long dinosaur-like beast with a huge humped back, long neck, and small head. In 1994, a famous photograph of the Loch Ness Monster was proven to be a fake.
Yeti (or Abominable Snowman)	Himalayan Mountains (India, Tibet, and Nepal)	In 1921, English explorers in the Himalayas found enormous human footprints. This led people to believe that a Yeti—a giant ape-like creature covered with hair that searches at night for its victims—existed.

BELIEVE IT OR NOT, THESE CREATURES ARE REAL!

Creature	Where You'll Find It	The Story
Tasmanian Devil	Tasmania (island off the coast of Australia) 	This black-colored, carnivorous mammal was called a "devil" for its screech. When threatened, the Tasmanian devil opens its mouth up wide, showing its large fangs. The two-foot-long animal is fierce, and hunts for animals bigger than itself, like small kangaroos, lizards, and rodents. Once almost extinct, now it's a protected animal.
Okapi	The Congo (Central Africa)	This looks like a mythical creature—a cross between an antelope, a donkey, and a zebra. Its coat is reddish brown, its thighs are striped white and purplish-black, and it has ears longer than a donkey. The Okapi is related to the giraffe.
Komodo Dragon	Indonesia (Southeast Asia) 	Thought dragons were the stuff of fairy tales? Not this one! The Komodo dragon is the largest lizard in the world, growing up to ten feet long. The dragons were discovered in the early 1900s, and are only found on a few small islands in Indonesia. These lizards like to lounge during the day, but they can run as fast as a dog when they need to. They feed on small animals, eggs, and sometimes even deer and pigs.

How Well Do You Know Where Things Come From?

You've heard the expression, "the greatest thing since sliced bread" before, right? What's that all about? Sure, sliced bread makes putting together sandwiches (another invention you'll soon read about) a lot simpler. But was it *really* so difficult to take out a knife and cut off a piece of bread before 1928 (when Otto Frederick Rohwedder invented the world's first mechanical bread slicer)? You be the judge, and decide how difficult life would be without any of these amazing inventions!

WHAT CAME FIRST?

Can you put these life-changing inventions of the last 200 years in the correct order (from oldest—1805—to most recent—1973)?

1805	Automobile
1843	Vacuum cleaner
1858	Can opener
1876	Internet
1889	Refrigerator
1901	Fax machine
1927	Telephone
1935	Television
1948	Ballpoint pen
1973	Velcro

Answers

1805: Refrigerator, 1843: Fax machine, 1858: Can opener, 1876: Telephone, 1889: Automobile, 1901: Vacuum cleaner, 1927: Television, 1935: Ballpoint pen, 1948: Velcro, 1973: Internet

YOU ARE WHAT YOU INVENT!

Some of the world's inventions have some tasty stories to go with them! Which one's your favorite?

1762: THE SANDWICH

Ever wonder where this lunchtime favorite came from? Well, the story is that the sandwich was invented around 1762 by John Montagu, the fourth Earl of Sandwich, in England. The Earl was too busy for a proper meal, so he asked his cook to put some meat inside two slices of bread, and the sandwich was born. (Too bad peanut butter wasn't around then!)

1886: COCA-COLA

Coca-Cola was invented by Dr. John Pemberton, a pharmacist from Atlanta, Georgia, who came up with the secret formula in a kettle in his backyard. By the end of the century, Coca-Cola became one of the most popular fountain drinks in America, and eventually around the world!

1896: THE ICE CREAM CONE

Even though Italian immigrant Italo Marchiony is given credit for inventing the ice cream cone (and got a patent, which gave him control over his invention, in 1903), another discovery took place

around the same time during a fair in 1904. Charles Menches, an ice cream vendor, sold his ice cream in dishes, like everyone else did at that time. But when he ran out of dishes one day, he looked over to another stand, where his friend was selling a wafer-like pastry. Menches rolled up the pastry, topped it with his ice cream, and—yum—the first ice cream cone was born!

1905: THE POPSICLE

An 11-year-old kid invented this luscious lick-able treat by accident! One day, Frank Epperson mixed some drink powder and water together and left it on his back porch with a stir stick in it overnight. The mixture froze, and the next day he had the very first popsicle! Epperson waited eighteen years to go into business selling the sticks, which he first called "Epsicles," a combination of his name and the word *icicle*. The name was eventually changed to "popsicle," and now millions are sold each year!

1912: LIFE SAVERS

LIFE PRESERVER

Do you know what a life saver is? It's an old-fashioned life preserver that was used on ships to throw to anyone who fell overboard. Clarence Crane used the name for his unique round mints with a hole in the middle. He invented them in 1912, when he decided to use a drug store pill-making machine to make a new-shaped mint (in those days most mints were square). To make them even more unique, he punched a hole in the middle by hand.

1921: WHEATIES

Thanks to advertising, this cereal has long been known as the "Breakfast of Champions." But how was this cereal invented? By accident! In 1921, a health worker was cooking up some bran for his patients. A little mix fell onto the hot stove, where it sizzled and baked into a crispy flake. The worker took his creation to a company where a man named George Cormack developed a sturdier flake (after testing 36 varieties of wheat!) that wouldn't crumble in the box. The company held a contest to come up with a name for the new cereal, and "Wheaties" was chosen over "Nutties" and "Gold Medal Wheat Flakes."

1928: BUBBLE GUM

Another accidental discovery that was almost too good to be *chewed* was bubble gum! It was invented by Walter E. Diemer. Diemer worked as an accountant back in 1928 for a chewing gum company in Philadelphia. In his spare time, he played around with new gum recipes, and came up with a gum that was less sticky and stretchier than regular chewing gum. Double Bubble was created, and sold at a penny a piece. Diemer himself taught salespeople how to blow bubbles—and he eventually became senior vice president of the company.

By George, I've Got It!

Think you need to be a genius, or at least a grown-up, to invent stuff? Well, as you just read, the person who invented the popsicle was only 11 years old. Check out some other stuff invented by kids—when they were all under 16!

- A fold-away step stool for kids (5 years old)
- An edible pet spoon (6 years old)
- A lighted mailbox (9 years old)
- A no-spill pet-feeding bowl (11 years old)

- A baseball glove and bat carrier (12 years old)
- A remote-control fish feeder (12 years old)
- Earmuffs (15 years old)
- Electric Christmas lights (15 years old)

How Well Do You Know the English Language?

Yeah, you've been speaking English since you were a tot. You've probably been studying its grammar and spelling more than you want to! But the truth is, languages are like *living* things—they grow and change all the time. The English language, like any other, has been through a lot of changes over the years. Are you an English *know-it-all*? Here's a chance to test your skills!

SONA SI LATINE LOQUERIS!

Say *what*? That means, "Honk if you speak Latin!" *Who in the world speaks Latin?* you might ask. Well—how about *you*? It's true! You speak more Latin than you know—check it out.

Latin is an ancient language that was spoken by the Romans way back in time. As the Romans conquered Europe, they took their language with them, and it eventually evolved into a bunch of other languages, like French, Spanish, Italian, and Portuguese, which all have Latin roots and similar words.

So, what does all this have to do with you and *English*, which isn't even a Latin-based language? Well, Latin snuck into the English language through *French*. In 1066, England was conquered by French speakers, and for the next 600 years or so, *French* became the official language of *England*. During that time, English borrowed bunches of words from French, which never lost its Latin influence. In fact, experts estimate that as much as 60 percent of the English vocabulary comes from French (more on this later)! Other Latin words were borrowed directly by scientists, scholars, and religious folk who felt that Latin was a more perfect language than English. Through all this, Latin made its place in the English language, where it still rolls off your tongue today, whether you realize it or not!

Today, Latin words are found everywhere in English. Some of these take the form of Latin prefixes—the beginning parts of words that change their meanings (like *pre-*, *re-*, and *de-*). Take the Pre-fix It! quiz and see if you can figure out what the words below mean, based on their Latin prefixes!

POP QUIZ — **PRE-FIX IT!**

1. If *coauthor* means "to write something together" (co- + author), which word using the prefix *co-* means "to live together"?

    a. costar

    b. cohabitate

    c. coordinate

2. If *subsoil* means "underground" (sub- + soil), which word using the prefix *sub-* means "underwater"?

    a. subhuman

    b. substandard

    c. submarine

3. If *rewrite* means "to write something again" (re- + write), which word using the prefix *re-* means "to make something again"?

    a. rebuild

    b. return

    c. rerun

4. If *international* means "between nations" (inter- + national), what word using the prefix *inter-* means "between people"?

    a. interdependent

    b. interpersonal

    c. interruption

5. If *deactivate* means "to turn something off" (de- + activate), what word using the prefix *de-* means "to thaw something"?

    a. decompress

    b. decompose

    c. defrost

6. If *prepay* means "to pay for something first" (pre- + pay), what word using the prefix *pre-* means "to think of something first"?

    a. prearrange

    b. preconceive

    c. preamble

Answers 1. b, 2. c, 3. a, 4. b, 5. c, 6. b

IT'S ALL GREEK TO ME!

As if Latin wasn't enough, English words also trace their roots to Greek, another popular ancient language. One Greek root that you're probably familiar with is "phobia," which means "an intense fear of a particular thing." Are you **claustrophobic** (which means you're afraid of closed or narrow spaces)? Or **decidophobic** (which means you're afraid of decisions)? Can't make up your mind? Well, see if you can decide what these different phobias mean, based on their roots. Match each name to the right fear.

1. Zoophobia

2. Triskaidekaphobia

3. Dentophobia

4. Pharmacophobia

5. Pyrophobia

6. Photophobia

7. Carnophobia

8. Arachnophobia

9. Technophobia

10. Testophobia

11. Hippopotomonstro-
sesquippedaliophobia

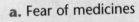
MY DOG IS SUPEREXTRAORDINARY!!!

a. Fear of medicines

b. Fear of animals

c. Fear of technology

d. Fear of long words

e. Fear of meat

f. Fear of the number 13

g. Fear of dentists

h. Fear of light

i. Fear of fire

j. Fear of taking tests

k. Fear of spiders

Answers

1. b, 2. f, 3. g, 4. a, 5. i, 6. h, 7. e, 8. k, 9. c, 10. j, 11. d

Now, see if you can guess what the names of these fears are!
Hint: they all end in "phobia"!

1. Fear of outer space _____

2. Fear of phobias _____

3. Fear of ideas _____

4. Fear of small things _____

5. Fear of time _____

6. Fear of strangers _____

7. Fear of ghosts _____

Answers

Is there anything that you have an intense fear of? Go ahead and name it! You can make up your very own phobia (unless you're phobophobic, of course!).

DO YOU SPEAK AMERICAN?

The folks who sailed here from England on the Mayflower in 1620 not only brought their hats and shoes, they brought their language, too! But a lot of the English spoken in America today (often called "American") includes words from a bunch of *other* cultures from around the world. Can you guess which ones?

1. The words *raccoon, canoe, barbeque, moccasin,* and *squash* (other possible words include *powwow, totem,* and *opossum*) come from:

   a. Irish

   b. Native American languages

   c. Chinese

2. The words *rodeo, macho, tuna, tango, fiesta,* and *armadillo* come from:

   a. French

   b. Native American languages

   c. Spanish

3. The words *jambalaya, bayou,* and *armoire* come from:

   a. West African languages

   b. Spanish

   c. French

4. The words *zen, karaoke, haiku,* and *karate* come from:

   a. Chinese

   b. Japanese

   c. Portuguese

5. The words *chop suey, kumquat, soy,* and *tea* come from:

   a. Chinese

   b. Indian languages

   c. Japanese

Answers 1. b, 2. c, 3. c, 4. b, 5. a

49

PARDON MY FRENCH

Do you speak French? *Oui!* That is, *yes* (or at least a lot more than you *think* you do)! That's because the English language has borrowed *thousands* of words from French over the years (remember that little invasion business we mentioned earlier?). Test your skills with the Feeling Frenchy? quiz! Match each French word to what it means in English.

I'M GOING TO RENDEZVOUS WITH THE MAITRE D' TO SEE IF I CAN SCORE SOME HORS D'OEUVRES

POP QUIZ — FEELING FRENCHY?

1. **rendezvous**
   (pronounced *ron-day-voo*)

2. **hors d'oeuvre**
   (pronounced *or-derv*)

3. **déjà vu**
   (pronounced *day-ja-voo*)

4. **maitre d'**
   (pronounced *mater-dee*)

5. **a la mode**
   (pronounced just like it looks!)

6. **chic**
   (pronounced *sheek*)

7. **entrepreneur**
   (pronounced *on-tra-pra-newer*)

8. **bon vivant**
   (pronounced *bon vi-von*)

9. **au contraire**
   (pronounced *oh con-trair*)

10. **souvenir**
    (pronounced *soo-ven-ear*)

a. on the contrary

b. a business person

c. a meeting

d. with ice cream

e. an appetizer

f. a host in a restaurant

g. fashionable

h. a memory

i. someone who enjoys life

j. a feeling that you've done the same thing before

Answers

1. **c.** A meeting, as in, "I don't like to think of it as detention, but as a little **rendezvous** with the assistant principal!"

2. **e.** An appetizer, as in "Are pizza rolls fancy enough to be **hors d'oeuvres**, or should we just call them 'snacks'?"

3. **j.** A feeling that you've done the same thing before, as in "This is total **déjà vu**, Mom—I could've sworn we had this for dinner last night!"

4. **f.** A host in a restaurant, as in, "Do you think the **maitre d'** could get us a better table? This one is practically in the bathroom!"

5. **d.** With ice cream, as in, "Could I get my broccoli **a la mode**?"

6. **g.** Fashionable, as in, "You may think it's **chic** to wear fur, but it looks like that coat *ate* you!"

7. **b.** A business person, as in, "It's tough being an **entrepreneur** when no one wants lemonade in December!"

8. **i.** Someone who enjoys life, as in, "I'm trying to be a **bon vivant**, but school gets in the way!"

9. **a.** On the contrary, as in, "**Au contraire**, you did take the last doughnut—I saw you eat it!"

10. **h.** A memory, as in, "I hope you like the **souvenir** I brought you—it's toilet paper from the hotel we stayed at in France!"

WHERE'S THE LOO?

How would you answer that question? Did you know that the "loo" means "bathroom" in England? Well, it's a good thing to know, in case you ever find yourself in the motherland of the English language, and can't hold it in! Believe it or not, even though you *think* you speak English, you'd be surprised to hear how different folks in England sound. Take the Queen's English quiz and see how you'd fare without a translator!

POP QUIZ **QUEEN'S ENGLISH**

1. If you ask for some "chips" in England, you should expect to get:

    a. your favorite brand of potato chips in a bag

    b. a pile of pieces of wood

    c. french fries

2. If you call something "brilliant" in England, you're saying that it's:

    a. super-smart

    b. super-stupid

    c. awesome, cool, or just great

3. If someone asks you where's the "queue," they're looking for:

    a. the letter "q"

    b. a mailbox

    c. the line

4. If you're lost and ask where to find your street, and someone says, "over by that lorry," you should look for a:

    a. young girl

    b. tall building

    c. truck

5. If someone asks you to put your "sarnie in the boot," they're asking you to:

    a. put your foot in the shoe

    b. put your sock on your foot

    c. put your sandwich in the trunk

6. If you overhear a British mother talking to her baby about his "nappy," she's referring to his:

    a. blanky

    b. pacifier

    c. diaper

How'd You Do?

Give yourself one point for every **c** you chose. If you got a score of 5 points or more, you're a **Brilliant Brit**! If you got 2 to 4 points, you are **Somewhat Smashing** (which by the way, means "great")! If you got a score of 1 point or less, well—then you're just an **American**!

Try playing *Word Sense* using different languages, like French, Spanish, or British English!

ARE YOU A PROVERB PRO?

Would you rather *chew the fat, blow smoke,* or *roll with the punches*? Not sure? Well, believe it or not, all of these popular expressions, known as **proverbs**, have real meanings, whether they make sense at first or not! Proverbs come from all over the place—from farming tips ("make hay while the Sun shines") to Shakespeare ("absence makes the heart grow fonder"). Wherever they came from, these little pearls of wisdom make the English language more colorful—and at times, more confusing! And every proverb has its own wacky history, which you, as the proverb know-it-all, will soon discover. Take the Proverb Pro quiz on the next page and see how *practice makes perfect*!

1. If someone says, "close, but no cigar," they mean:

   a. you have no idea what you're talking about

   b. you should stop smoking because it's bad for your health

   c. you're almost there, but not a winner

2. If your mom says, "don't look a gift horse in the mouth," she means:

   a. you should be careful around big animals

   b. you shouldn't be ungrateful

   c. you need to brush your teeth

3. If you "have an axe to grind," you:

   a. are looking for trouble

   b. have a secret motive

   c. have a point to make

4. If you have a "knee-jerk reaction" to something, you're:

   a. acting like a jerk

   b. responding to something automatically

   c. hurting your knee

5. If your next-door neighbor says he's "busting your chops," he's:

   a. threatening to beat you up

   b. making you laugh really hard

   c. giving you a hard time

6. If your friend asks if you want to "chew the fat," he wants to:

   a. take you out to dinner

   b. give you a piece of gum

   c. chat about nothing important

7. If you're going to "hit the hay," you're going to:

    a. go to bed

    b. fall down

    c. get really mad

8. If your teacher says to stop "blowing smoke," she means:

    a. stop smoking

    b. stop saying stuff that isn't true

    c. stop waving your arms around

9. If your dad says you should "roll with the punches," he means you should:

    a. roll with your hands in a fist

    b. go along with something

    c. get moving in a hurry

Answers

1. c. When you come close to success, someone could say that you're "close, but no cigar"—which refers to old-time slot machines and carnival games that gave cigars as prizes!

2. b. "Looking a gift horse in the mouth" refers to counting a horse's teeth to tell its age. If it were a gift, this would be impolite, because you should be grateful for any kind of horse (or gift), no matter how old it is!

3. c. It sounds more threatening than it is, but "having an axe to grind" is having a point to make. You want to make your point clear, and make it work for you, just like grinding an axe makes it sharper.

4. b. Having a "knee-jerk reaction" means to have an automatic response to something, and refers to the reflex in your knee. Try it—if your leg is hanging still off a chair, tap your knee lightly and watch it kick out automatically! A doctor might tap your knee with a rubber hammer to check your reflexes.

5. c. A long time ago, it was fashionable for men to wear long sideburns, called "mutton" or "lamb chops." A "bust in the chops" used to mean getting hit in the face. Now, the expression means to get insulted or harassed, but in a friendly way.

6. **c.** A group of people similar to Eskimos used to chew on whale blubber to pass the time (kind of like the gum you chew today). "Chewing the fat" refers to talking about nothing important to pass the time.

7. **a.** In old times, mattresses were stuffed with hay, so "hitting the hay" was actually going to bed.

8. **b.** A person who's "blowing smoke" is trying to make you believe something that might not be true, or doesn't know what he's talking about and is covering it up. This saying comes from magicians, who sometimes use smoke in their performances to make it harder for the audience to see their tricks.

9. **b.** In boxing, when someone moves away from a punch to avoid it, or make it less powerful, it's called "rolling with the punches." The expression also refers to going along with something, rather than fighting it.

KNOW YOUR "-ONYMS"

The English language has a whole lot of words that end in –onym (which comes from the Greek word *onyma*, or "name"). That is, words ending in "onym" are names for types of words! Be an -onym know-it-all!

ACRONYMS

Words or names that are formed by putting together the first letters from a phrase, like **ASAP** (which stands for **A**s **S**oon **A**s **P**ossible), **FAQs** (**F**requently **A**sked **Q**uestions), or **BLT** (**B**acon, **L**ettuce, and **T**omato) are called acronyms. With online chatting, acronyms are more popular than ever, since they cut down the number of keys you need to type. Do you know the meaning of these popular acronyms?

> **a.** LOL   **b.** TTYL   **c.** BFN   **d.** GTG   **e.** FYI

Answers

a. laughing out loud, **b.** talk to you later, **c.** bye for now, **d.** got to go, **e.** for your information

SYNONYMS

Words that have the same meaning, like *funny* and *hilarious*, *gross* and *disgusting*, or *huge* and *enormous*.

ANTONYMS

Words with opposite meanings, like *gigantic* and *puny*, *tidy* and *messy*, and *crunchy* and *soggy*.

Gigantic

EEEK!

Puny

APTRONYMS

Names that fit what people do for a living, like *Dr. Aiken Head* for a head doctor, *Ms. Rita Book* for a librarian, *Mr. Bill Bord* for a sign painter, *Dr. Seymour* for an optometrist, *Ms. Sue Yoo* for a lawyer, or *Noah Lott* for a know-it-all like you! Come up with your own funny aptronyms that would fit a teacher, dentist, or any other job you can think of!

WHAT'S 8 × 3, NOAH LOTT?

UH... I DUNNO!

CAPITONYMS

Words that change meaning and pronunciation depending on whether they are capitalized or not, like "polish" (*pol*-ish—to rub something shiny) and "Polish" (*Po*-lish—someone from Poland), or "nice" (a positive adjective) and "Nice" (pronounced *niece*, a city in France).

HETERONYMS

Words that have the same spelling, but entirely different meanings and pronunciation, like the word "bow" (think "bow" in "bow and arrow," versus to "take a bow").

PSEUDONYMS

Fake or pen names used by authors like Theodor Geisel, who used the name "Dr. Seuss" on his books.

HOMONYMS

Words that sound the same when you say them but have different spellings and meanings, like "right" and "write," "ant" and "aunt," and "bored" and "board." (They're also called "homophones.")

I ATE ANTS WITH MY AUNT AT EIGHT...

ICK!

Can You Make a Pear?

Oops, meant to say a "pair"! Sometimes English can get pretty confusing! Can you come up with another word that sounds the same as each one below, but has a different spelling and meaning (like *raise* and *rays*)? If so, then you'll be a master **homonym** maker!

1. chews _____(to select)

2. beat _____(a purplish vegetable)

3. whale_____(a type of cry)

4. sent _____(a smell)

5. heal _____(a part of the foot)

6. peace_____(a part)

7. discussed _____(a sickening feeling)

8. bare_____(a large mammal)

9. wrap _____(a type of music)

10. role _____(to flip over)

11. steel _____(to take without asking)

NAME THAT SOUND!

Onomatopoeia is a long (and really hard-to-spell) word for something pretty simple—the burps, slurps, honks, buzzes, hisses, and everything else you hear around you. That is, they're the words that describe the sounds you hear. But not all words that refer to noises are onomatopoeias—only the ones that actually *sound* like them. Can you tell the difference? Which of the following words are onomatopoeias?

bang	vacuum	type	gulp	squeak
splash	scrape	flip	slap	whisper
shout	whirr	fall	tinkle	smack
mix	drop	weep	swoosh	wham

Answers

meyм 'ʞɔɐɯs
'ʞɐǝnbs 'ɥsooмs 'ǝlʞuıʇ 'dlnɓ 'ɹɹıɥм 'ɥsɐlds 'ɓuɐq

Barks Around the World

Do dogs sound the same in China, or do they speak a different bark? You decide! People that speak English usually refer to a dog's barking sounds as "woof," "bow wow," or "ruff ruff." Check out how onomatopoeias can change, depending on where you live, and how dogs "sound" in other languages!

Arabic: haw haw	**German:** wau wau	**Japanese:** wanwan, kyankyan
Bengali: ghaue-ghaue	**Greek:** gav	
Catalan: bup, bup	**Hindi:** bho bho	**Korean:** mung-mung
Chinese: wang wang	**Hungarian:** vau vau	**Russian:** gav-gav
Dutch: woef	**Icelandic:** voff	**Swedish:** vov vov
Estonian: auh	**Indonesian:** gonggong	**Turkish:** hav hav
French: ouah ouah	**Italian:** bau bau	**Ukrainian:** haf-haf
		Vietnamese: wau wau

CAN YOU READ BACKWARDS?

You can—if you're reading a **palindrome**! That's because palindromes are words that read the same forward or backward, like **noon**, **bib**, **did**, **madam**, or **ewe** (quick—do you know what a *ewe* is?). You can also make palindrome sentences, like "Was it a rat I saw?" or "Todd erases a red dot."

Figure out which of the sentences below are palindromes, and which ones are just weird combinations of words!

1. A Toyota
2. Bob has a job
3. Madam, I'm Adam
4. A Santa at NASA
5. Water warts grow
6. A daffodil slid off Ada
7. Stressed no desserts
8. Evil olive
9. A nut for a jar of tuna
10. Knock knock

Answers

Numbers 1, 3, 4, 6, 8, and 9 are palindromes.

Know-It-All Fact!

KINNIKINNIK is the longest palindrome word in English! What does it mean? According to Webster's dictionary, it's "a mixture used by North American Indians as a substitute for tobacco, or for mixing with it; the commonest ingredients are dried sumac leaves and the inner bark of dogwood or willow." Who knew?

READY FOR SOME SERIOUS FUN?

Did you notice what's odd about the heading "serious fun"? It's an **oxymoron**! Settle down, there's no name-calling going on here! Oxymorons, as insulting as they may *sound*, are simply words with opposite meanings (that would normally contradict each other) put together. Can you figure out the other half of these popular oxymoronic expressions?

1. bad _____

2. pretty _____

3. definite _____

4. jumbo _____

ARE YOU A SPELLING KNOW-IT-ALL?

Before you answer "yes," take this test of commonly misspelled words and see how you do!

Is It:

1. a. seperate　　　　or　　　　**b.** separate

2. a. irresistible　　　or　　　　**b.** irrestisable

3. a. receive　　　　or　　　　**b.** recieve

4. a. weird　　　　　or　　　　**b.** wierd

5. a. independent　　or　　　　**b.** independant

6. a. occasion　　　　or　　　　**b.** ocassion

7. a. brocolli　　　　or　　　　**b.** broccoli

How Well Do You Know the Final Frontier?

Space—there's no place like it on Earth—literally! What's out there in the vast blackness in the sky? How familiar are you with our galaxy, including the Sun, Moon, and other stuff? Well, it's time to find out! Not only do you need to be a space know-it-all to impress your friends, family, and score a stellar grade in science class— you'll want to know more about what just might be your future home someday!

WHY DOES IT WORK LIKE THAT?

The Sun goes up and down every day, and the Moon takes its place at night—how and why does all that happen? Can you match the right explanation of what happens in space with each question?

1. Why does the Sun rise and set each day?

    a. As the Sun and Earth orbit each other, it looks like the Sun rises and sets in the sky.

    b. The Earth rotates on an axis, which makes the Sun seem like it's the one moving around.

2. Why does the Moon change shape over the course of a month?

    a. The Moon isn't perfectly round, so as it orbits the Earth we see it from different angles.

    b. As the Moon orbits the Earth, we see different amounts of it that are lit by the Sun, versus parts that are in shadow.

3. Why do you feel hot in the summer?

    a. Your part of the Earth is closer to the Sun than during the winter.

    b. The tilt of the Earth on its axis makes the Sun's rays more direct in the summer than in the winter.

4. Why don't you fly off Earth into space?

    a. The Earth's ozone layer traps the atmosphere—and you—on the planet.

    b. The Earth's gravitational pull gets you, and everything else, to stay put.

5. Why don't the Sun's rays burn you to a crisp?

    a. You always wear sunblock, and the Sun is really far away.

    b. The Earth's atmosphere has shields that protect you from UV light and radiation from the Sun.

6. Why doesn't the Earth bump into other planets in space?

    a. The Earth has a protective shield around it that deflects any moving objects from getting too close.

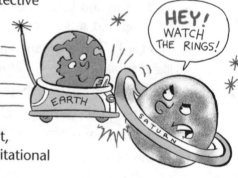

HEY! WATCH THE RINGS!

EARTH

SATURN

    b. The Earth is firmly locked in orbit, trapped by the gravitational pull of the Sun.

WHAT'S A REAL STAR?

You follow their Hollywood careers, jam to their music, marvel at their slam dunks—but those everyday celebrity chumps have *nothing* on the real stars that rock the universe! What do you know about the billions of stars that light up the night sky, and the superstar that keeps life on our planet going (that would be the Sun, in case you're wondering!)? Take the Star Search! quiz and see!

POP QUIZ — **STAR SEARCH!**

1. The stars in space are made out of:

   a. chunks of rock that reflect light, like the Moon

   b. glowing balls of hot gases

   c. tiny particles of stardust

2. Stars come in different colors, depending on their temperatures:

   a. the hottest stars are blue or white, and the coolest are red

   b. the hottest stars are red, and the coolest are blue or white

   c. the hottest stars are the most popular

3. The Sun is:

   a. a gigantic star

   b. an average-sized star

   c. a pee-wee star

4. The Sun has enough energy to burn for:

   a. 2 million more years

   b. 5 billion more years

   c. forever

5. When an average-sized star runs out of energy, it:

a. becomes a burnt-out lump in space

b. explodes

c. gets absorbed by an asteroid

6. The Sun is the biggest thing in our solar system. In fact, it's:

a. bigger than all the planets and moons in it combined

b. bigger than 100 Earths put together

c. bigger than 10 Earths put together

7. The light that you feel from the Sun takes:

a. 20 minutes to travel from the surface of the Sun to Earth

b. eight minutes to travel from the surface of the Sun to Earth

c. one millisecond, or so little time it's almost instant

8. The Sun's solar flares refer to:

a. violent explosions of gases exploding from the surface of the Sun

b. mini-stars that hang around the Sun

c. the rays of light that seem to extend beyond the Sun itself

Check your answers on the next page and give yourself **one point** for every answer you get correct. Rate yourself!

6–8 points: **Shining Star!**

3–5 points: **Star Light!**

0–2 points: **Star Struck!**

Answers

1. **b.** Stars are giant balls of hot gas, mostly hydrogen and helium.

2. **a.** Just like hot charcoal in a barbecue grill, the hottest stars are blue or white.

3. **b.** The Sun is average-sized.

4. **b.** No need to worry about the Sun running out of gas any time soon!

5. **a.** When an average-sized star dies, it takes a couple billion years for it to finally become a lump of nothing.

6. **a.** The Sun is bigger than everything in the solar system combined. You could pour 1.3 million Earths into the Sun!

7. **b.** The light you feel on your face takes eight minutes to get through space from the Sun!

8. **a.** Solar flares are violent explosions that happen from time to time on the Sun's surface, releasing huge amounts of energy (we're talking serious rays here!) into the universe. They can harm astronauts and space equipment, and even cause power outages all the way on Earth!

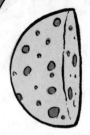

A HUNK OF GREEN CHEESE

Long ago, before anyone ever explored the Moon up close, some people believed it was made out of green cheese. Can you figure out if these statements about the Moon are true or just "cheesy" false?

YUM!

1. The Moon is about a quarter of the size of Earth.

2. The Moon glows because of an energy source inside it.

3. The Moon is mostly made of rock.

4. There are enormous telescopes on the Moon that listen for signals from aliens.

5. The dark and light spots you see on the Moon are shadows.

6. The Moon is covered with a powdery substance.

7. No person has ever walked on the Moon.

8. The Moon has thousands of craters of all shapes and sizes.

9. The Moon has a dark side that no one has ever seen.

10. The "Man in the Moon" refers to the alien people we think live in the Moon.

I'M THE MAN!

MAN IN THE MOON

Answers

1. **True.** The Moon is so big compared to the moons orbiting other planets that Earth is sometimes called a *double* planet (our Moon is bigger than the entire planet Pluto!). Jupiter has more than 60 moons that have been discovered so far, but most of them are smaller than our Moon.

2. **False.** The Moon glows because it reflects light from the Sun.

3. **True.** Even though some people used to think it was made of green cheese, the Moon is made of solid rock, including many of the same minerals that you find on Earth.

4. **False.** Not yet! That's a possibility for the future. The Moon is a great place to listen for signals in space. It's just that funds aren't being spent to develop these kinds of telescopes.

5. **False.** The dark and light spots on the Moon are caused by different materials on its surface.

6. **True.** The Moon has a powdery substance covering it called "regolith" (better known as "moondust") that feels like flour and doesn't ever blow away since there's no wind up there.

7. **False.** Twelve astronauts have walked on the Moon. The first was Neil Armstrong back in 1969.

8. **True.** No one knows for sure where the craters came from, but scientists think they're from meteors slamming into the Moon's surface.

9. **False.** It's true that there is a side of the Moon that we never see from Earth, but it's not dark! Its more accurate name is the "far side" of the Moon, and it's been viewed by satellites.

10. **False.** The "Man in the Moon" is a nickname for the light and dark pattern on the Moon that many people think looks like a face.

IS THERE ANYBODY OUT THERE?

That's the multi-billion-dollar question humans have been trying to answer forever! Since 1965, when we Earthlings got our first close-up photos of Mars, we've been wondering whether there are any life forms out there. Not walking, talking, UFO-flying, helmet-wearing Martians. More like the primitive stuff that's growing in the back of your refrigerator, or on the walls of your fish tank! Over the past few decades, scientists have found signs that could suggest something once lived on Mars, but there's no conclusive evidence of life anywhere else in the solar system—yet!

How do you find life on Mars?

Well, the thing to look for is *water*. On Earth, where you find water, you find life. That's why scientists today are looking for any evidence of water (like dried-up riverbeds, or underground water). So far, they've only found evidence that Mars held water in the past—so there may once have been life on the planet!

So, what are space know-it-alls doing to find the answers to their questions? Well, in 2003, NASA launched two Mars Exploration Rovers (called Spirit and Opportunity) that landed on

the planet in January 2004. The rovers are designed to study the history of water on Mars and its landscape. So far, it seems like Mars is an unfriendly place for any life forms to survive. If any have—and we find them— they'll probably look a *lot* different than anything we've seen before. What do *you* think?

Do Pigs Fly?

In space they can—but they haven't been there yet! Here's a sample of some of the many animals that *have* already gone into orbit:

- Dogs
- Monkeys
- Rabbits
- Fish
- Rats
- Jellyfish
- Fruit flies
- Hornets
- Tortoises

IS THE SPACE STATION A GIANT PLAY STATION?

Not at all, but astronauts on the International Space Station (ISS)—a permanent home for astronauts up in space, and a way for researchers to study the effects of long-term space living—*can* play video games, watch movies, and eat upside down as they float around in weightlessness!

Astronauts have been living up there since the year 2000 (for as long as six months at a time). Be a space station know-it-all with these cool facts:

- The ISS was built one section (or module) at a time, and carried into orbit by a space shuttle and other rockets! The first two modules were flown into space and connected in 1998, and since then, the space station has been continuously growing. More than 40 spaceflights will be needed to complete the station.

- The ISS is still being added to, and when it's done, it should be the length of a football field!

- The space station can be seen with the naked eye as it orbits 200 miles above Earth. (It looks like a slowly moving star!)

- The astronauts who live on board the space station see the Sun rise 16 times in 24 hours!

- Crew members sleep strapped into a sleeping bag to keep from floating away!

- Astronauts living on the ISS can't take a shower—instead, they take sponge baths and use a special no-rinse shampoo!

- The toilets on the space station don't have water, but work like vacuums that suck waste into a storage device!

- Astronauts who spend long periods of time in space lose bone and muscle from living in an environment with less gravity than Earth. That's why space station crew members work out hard with treadmills and resistance machines each day in space to make sure their bodies stay strong!

- Astronauts have to pick out what they want to eat for their entire stay before leaving Earth (it takes a *long* time to order delivery!). Plus, they can't have a soda for the whole time they're in space (since burping in space can make everything in your stomach come up—*yuck*)! What would *you* choose to eat for the next six months?

- The ISS is truly an international place. The astronauts living there have included Americans, Russians, Japanese, Canadians, and others!

WATCH OUT FOR FLYING TRASH!

Space is loaded with cool stuff like stars, moons, planets, and meteors. But did you know it's also full of **space junk**—trash that humans have dumped into the cosmos? No, not the nasty stuff that you toss into your garbage can, but 4 million pounds of old rocket parts, space stations, broken satellites, and more! Wondering why astronauts don't recycle? Well, they *try* to! But a certain amount of space junk can't be helped because, for example, it's too tough to track down an old satellite and bring it back to Earth. (ISS astronauts *do* send their trash back to Earth though, in case you were wondering!)

So what happens to this high-tech flying garbage in space? Well, if you're ever out there—watch out! It travels at super-speeds (try 17,500 miles per hour), and a piece that's as tiny as a quarter inch can damage the window of a space shuttle!

How Well Do You Know Money?

Money! It's one of those things that we use all the time but don't really stop to think about, or even notice. Take the Rolling in Dough quiz and see how you do!

POP QUIZ ▸ **ROLLING IN DOUGH**

1. Do you know what denominations (amounts) paper money comes in?

    a. $1, $5, $10, $20, $50, $100, and $500

    b. $1, $2, $5, $10, $20, $50, and $100

    c. $1, $2, $5, $10, $20, $50, $100, $500, $1,000, and $5,000

2. What is the official name for paper money in the United States?

    a. Promissory Notes

    b. Currency

    c. Federal Reserve Notes

3. What is the national motto of the United States that appears on dollars?

    a. In God We Trust

    b. Show Me the Money

    c. I Pledge Allegiance to the Flag

4. Which President appears on the U.S. penny?

    a. Abraham Lincoln

    b. Thomas Jefferson

    c. Franklin Roosevelt

5. Who appears on the U.S. $20 bill?

    a. George Washington

    b. Andrew Jackson

    c. Alexander Hamilton

Answers

1. b. The $2 bill is rare, but it exists! The $500, $1,000, and $5,000 denominations have not been printed since 1946.

2. c.

3. a.

4. a.

5. b.

Did You Know That...

- Each $1 bill you use for lunch money will wear out in about 17 months (that means that it'll be torn or faded so much by then that it won't be identifiable any more). Larger bills last longer, since they're used less frequently.

- If you stacked up all of the dollar bills worn out in one year, the pile would be 200 miles high! That's why the Bureau of Engraving and Printing runs its currency printing press day and night to print the several billion notes a year that are needed to keep up with the demand! The presses are in Washington, DC and in Fort Worth, Texas.

- It costs the same amount of money to make a $1 bill or a $100 bill—three cents!

- The paper used for printing money is a special mix of wood pulp and cotton. It's illegal for anyone to own any of this special currency paper.

- The U.S. Secret Service (yup, that's right, the same guys who protect the President) was established in 1865 to fight against counterfeit (fake) money. In that year, somewhere between a third and a half of all the paper money around was considered phony! But over the next ten years, that number dropped drastically as the Secret Service cracked down on counterfeiters.

SHOW ME THE MONEY!

Technology can lead to cool new stuff, but it can also lead to...fake money! High-tech photocopy machines, scanners, and ink-jet printers make it possible to create really convincing counterfeit money.

But to stop counterfeiters from getting too far, in 2003, the U.S. government introduced a new $20 bill, which hadn't had any major design changes since 1928! Check it out:

- **New watermark.** This faint image is a copy of the large presidential portrait on the front. If you hold the bill up to the light, you can see the watermark (which is part of the paper itself) on both sides.

- **Security thread.** This plastic strip is stuck in the paper and runs up one side. It glows green if you put it under an ultraviolet light!

- **Color-shifting ink.** If you tilt a new $20 bill up and down, the number "20" on the lower right corner will change color from copper to green.

- **Micro-printing.** Tiny yellow "20s" and black-lettered words, which are so small that they're hard to copy, appear on the new $20 bill. Can you find them?

- **More colors.** The old bill used to be only green and black, but the new $20 note has shades of peach, blue, and yellow.

- **New images.** There are new symbols of freedom on the bill, including American eagles. Plus, the portrait of President Andrew Jackson has changed.

What's more, the U.S. Treasury plans to update all the other denominations—*and* keep changing them every ten years to keep counterfeiters on their toes! Look out for the new money!

KEEP THE CHANGE!

Have you ever seen a French Franc, a Spanish Peseta, or a German Deutschmark? Better yet, do you *own* any coins from these or other European countries? If you do, hold on to them, because they might be worth more someday! That's because all of them—and other European currencies— were officially replaced in 2002 with a new currency called the **Euro**! The Euro works like the U.S. Dollar in that it has 100 cents. And now, each country in the European Union uses the same coins and bills, just like the American states do. The difference is that these are different *countries* sharing the same currency! A few countries are currently using *both* their traditional currency and the Euro, but over time, the old stuff will probably go out of style, or be too much of a pain to keep printing (so coin collectors, keep your eyes peeled!).

MONEY MAKES THE WORLD GO ROUND

Or it at least makes its way *around* the world! Are you a money know-it-all who can match these currencies to the countries that they come from?

1. Dollar   **A.** India

2. Peso   **B.** Russia

3. Colon   **C.** Mexico

4. Baht   **D.** Japan

5. Yen   **E.** Thailand

6. Kwacha   **F.** United States

7. Ruble   **G.** Malawi

8. Rupee   **H.** Costa Rica

Answers

1. F, 2. C, 3. H, 4. E, 5. D, 6. G, 7. B, 8. A

A Fool and His Money Are Soon Parted

Here are some other popular proverbs (remember those?) about money! How many of them have you heard before?

- Filthy rich

- Money doesn't grow on trees

- Take the money and run

- Put your money where your mouth is

- One for the money, two for the show

- Go for the gold

- Raking in the money

- Time is money

- Money talks

- A penny saved is a penny earned

- Right on the money

- In the money

Well, Whaddya Know!

So, here you are—at the end of the book. Are you ready to take on your newly earned know-it-all title with pride? Let's put it to the test: "So, when did you get to be such a know-it-all?" How does being called a know-it-all make you feel now? Super-smart? Proud of yourself? All-around great?

If so, that means you've officially transformed into the know-it-all we knew you could be! Think about it. How many other people do you know who could tell you how much spit you make in a lifetime, or what an okapi is? You've been around the world, through time and space, filling your brain with a ton of new knowledge! With all this information, you, our new know-it-all friend, are ready to survive just about any knowledge challenge out there. In the meantime, just remember that the best know-it-all brains thrive on more and more facts, tips, and trivia on just about everything. So, go put your new knowledge to work for you, and continue to learn, as you take on the *world*—no, make that the *universe*!